Creative Editions is an imprint of The Creative Company, 123 South Broad Street, Mankato, Minnesota 56001.
Library of Congress Cataloging-in-Publication Data
Les Chats Pelés.
[Vive la musique! English]
Long Live Music!/written and illustrated by Les Chats Pelés.
"Creative Editions."
This is a translation of: *Vive la musique!*
Summary: Presents a history of musical instruments beginning with the flute in about 40,000 B.C. and
including mention of pipes, trumpets, drums, opera, and jazz.
ISBN 0-15-201310-5
1. Music—History and criticism—Juvenile literature. [1. Music—History and criticism.]
I. Chats Pelés (Group of artists) II. Title.
ML3928.M3413 1996
780'.9—dc20   95-45739
Translation by Carol Volk.
Printed in Belgium   A B C D E
American edition designed by Stephanie Blumenthal

Hey, Pippo!
What happened
to you?

Silence the Giant smashed all my instruments! He's out to destroy music and me!

LONG LIVE MUSIC!

Written and Illustrated by

LES CHATS PELÉS

CREATIVE EDITIONS

MANKATO, MINNESOTA

HARCOURT BRACE & COMPANY

SAN DIEGO NEW YORK LONDON

Don't worry! we'll find all we need inside the big music book!

Rhythm!

rhythm marks time in music. We call it the beat. It makes us want to dance.

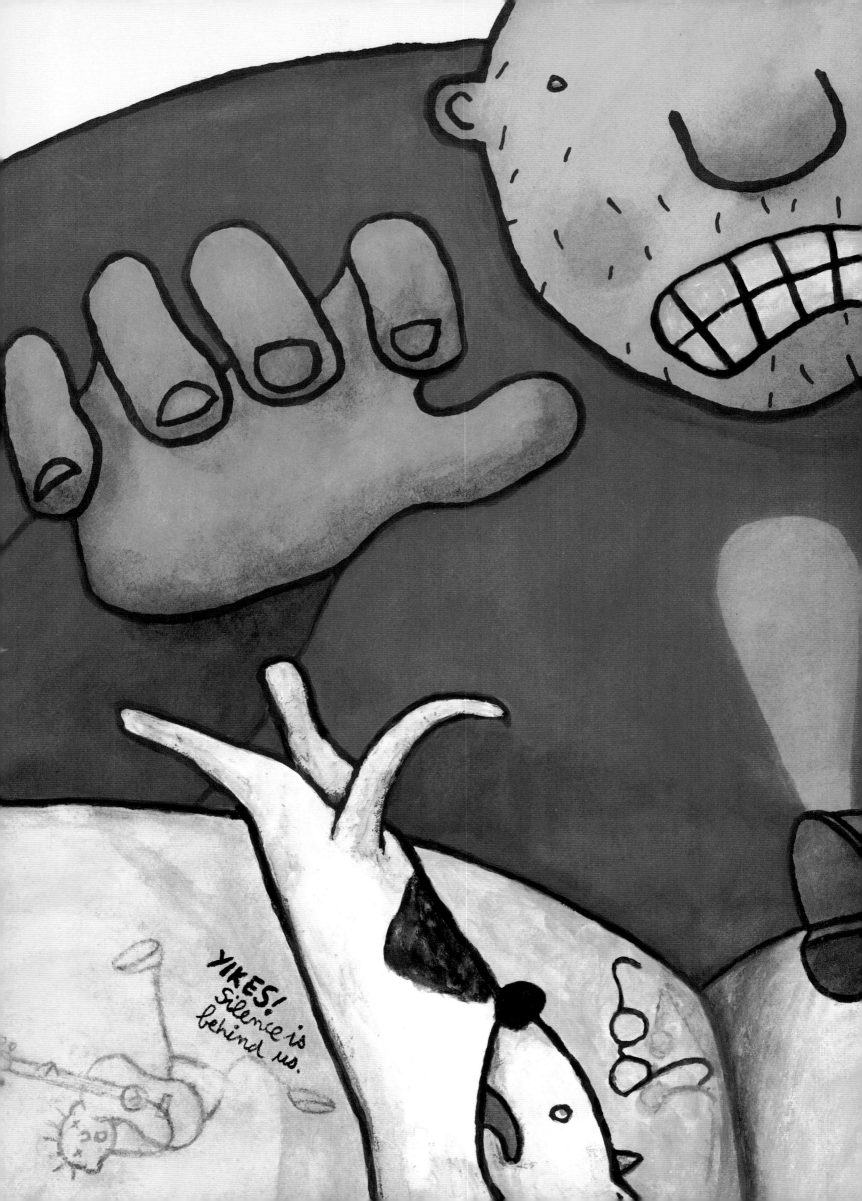

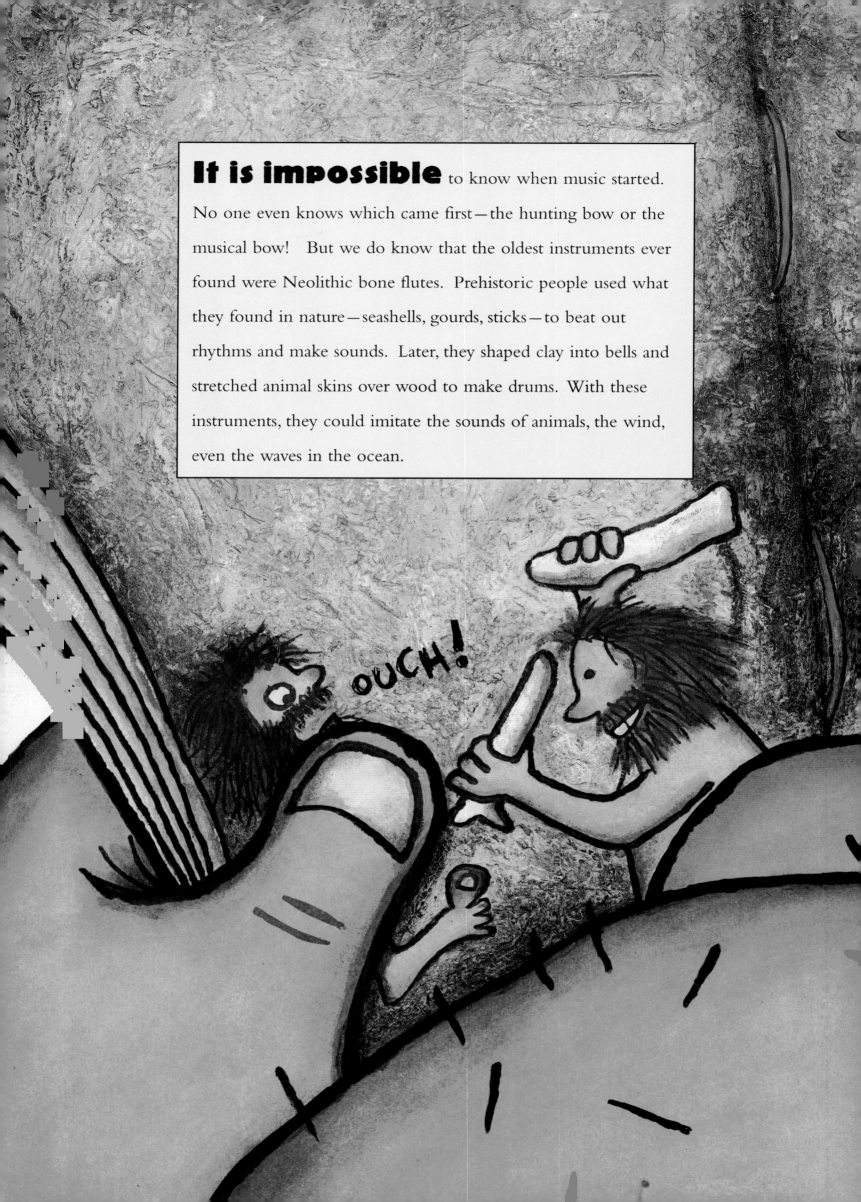

It is impossible to know when music started. No one even knows which came first—the hunting bow or the musical bow! But we do know that the oldest instruments ever found were Neolithic bone flutes. Prehistoric people used what they found in nature—seashells, gourds, sticks—to beat out rhythms and make sounds. Later, they shaped clay into bells and stretched animal skins over wood to make drums. With these instruments, they could imitate the sounds of animals, the wind, even the waves in the ocean.

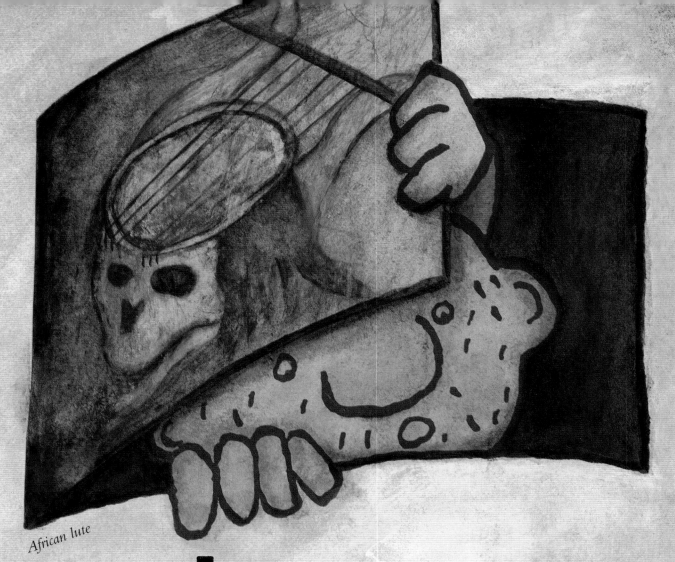

African lute

From China to Egypt, early civilizations

Pre-Columbian dancer

Celtic warrior trumpets

believed that music had magical powers.

bowed harp, lute, Egyptian harp, flute and double oboe

According to the Chinese and the Indians, it was a

Chinese mouth organ

detail of a Mesopotamian harp

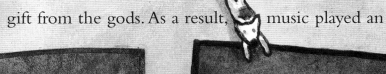
gift from the gods. As a result, music played an

frame drum and Assyrian lyre

important role in their religious ceremonies.

As the civilized world expanded, so did the role of music. Ships began sailing around the Mediterranean Sea and music traveled with them. In 500 B.C., the fun-loving Greeks surrounded themselves with sounds and songs in plays, dancing, poetry and even sports. Two important instruments for them were the *lyre*, a stringed instrument, and the *aulos*, a divided pipe instrument.

The fun was over in Greece when the Romans conquered their country! The Romans adopted all the Greek musical instruments. However, because the military spirit was so important to the Romans, they also developed big marching bands, with drums and trumpets, to inspire their soldiers. Nero, a Roman emperor who supposedly fiddled while Rome burned, might actually have been playing an instrument like a bagpipe called a *tibias*.

In the early Middle Ages (500-1000 A.D.), monks throughout Europe sang Gregorian chants in cathedrals. Except for organs, musical instruments were forbidden in church. As opposed to classical times, instruments were now thought to be the work of the devil.

But *jongleurs* or traveling musicians brought music to the people, performing in crowded city streets and in elegant castle halls. They juggled and did tricks with tame bears and often played a fiddle-like instrument called a *vielle*. Their long songs told of heroic deeds, stirring battles, and unrequited love. People listened to them when their day was over and they wanted to be entertained. By the end of the Middle Ages (1450 A.D.), music became more available as a system was devised to write down both the melody and the rhythm of music.

Bravo! Public theaters opened in Venice in the early 1600s and featured a new kind of stage play called the opera. Here the human voice took center stage, as all the words to these plays were sung. Operas were a thundering success. The baroque orchestras, which accompanied operas, were composed of stringed instruments, with the harpsichord acting as the rhythmic backbone. The violin came into its own in the late 1600s as Antonius Stradivarius made what many people still feel are the most perfect violins ever produced. The brass instruments, kettle drums, and the organ joined the orchestras for special occasions. By this time, thanks to the printing press, music traveled everywhere!

TIPS, PLEASE

Ta ta ta dum! These small baroque ensembles grew until, by the 1800s, they became symphony orchestras with over 100 instruments, including woodwinds, brass and percussion! Such famous composers as Schumann, Brahms and Dvorak wrote huge scores for these orchestras. The most famous symphony writer of all, Beethoven, composed some of his finest work while he was losing his hearing.

The piano entered the drawing-room scene in the early 1700s, while the accordion, the "poor man's piano," was very popular in the streets. The waltz took its first steps in Vienna; the tango lunged forward in Argentina. New instruments were being invented as new sounds were needed—Alfred Sax invented the saxophone in the mid–1800s.

While all this was happening in Europe, in the United States, blacks sang gospel and blues as they worked in the fields.

敬 馬 奇

The 20th century brought an amazing **explosion** of music. The radio, the record **player**, and the compact disc made music completely portable. **Music** has become inescapable. **It** surrounds us wherever we are.

¡QUE LOCURA!

CONCERT

фантастика!

C'est it's crazy

Jazz groups

start up in New Orleans and consist of a **rhythm** section:

stand-up bass or tuba

drums

guitar

banjo

and piano; and of a **m**elody section:

trombone

trumpet

saxophone

and clarinet

The beat goes on.

Rhythm 'n' blues, rock, ska, reggae, pop, funk, punk, rap...blast out all around us! At enormous concerts like Woodstock, amplified music blares out of huge speakers.

ziuNHiZZRRR

With synthesizers, a keyboard can sound like an orchestra! The earth turns and music goes along with it, always and everywhere. Long live all music!

Do you think anyone could ever stop music?

Hush, let's listen.

The Aerophones

Wind Instruments

Indian sringa horn

Roumanian pastoral horn

Serpent

Argentine horn

Russian zhaleyka

Pakistani flute

Ocarina

French horn

The Idiophones

Roumanian cymbals

New Guinea slit drum

Guinean sistrum

Central African mbira

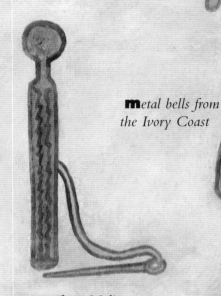

metal bells from
the Ivory Coast

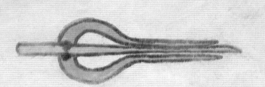

metal jew's harp from Rajasthan

Iron scraper from Mali

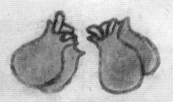

Spanish castanets

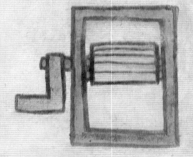

Moravian rattle

Brazilian
bull roarer

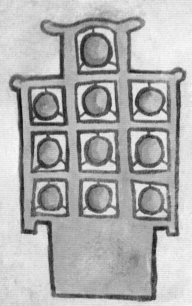

Chinese yunlou

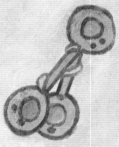

Moroccan metal castanets

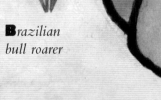

Cuban rattle

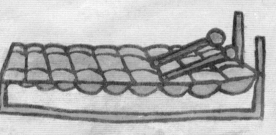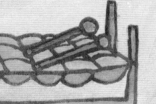

Xylophone from Mali

ukrainian bandore

The Chordophones

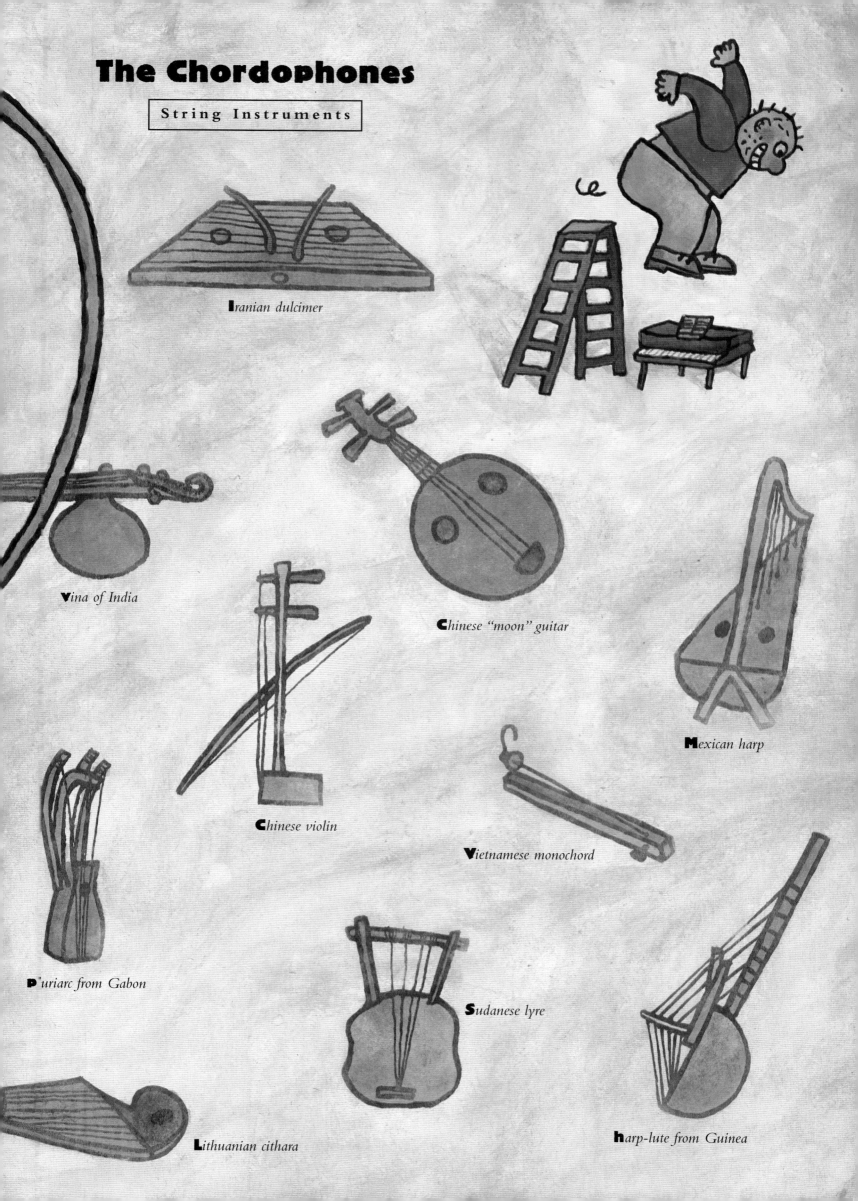

Iranian dulcimer

Vina of India

Chinese "moon" guitar

Chinese violin

Mexican harp

Vietnamese monochord

Puriarc from Gabon

Sudanese lyre

Lithuanian cithara

Harp-lute from Guinea

Congolese kettle drums

dhola drum from India

Orchestra kettle drum

Arab drum

Latin American congos

Argentine drums